Lifestyle Redesign

"Design the Life of your Dreams"

By
Temi Charlotte Oni

Lifestyle Redesign – "Design the Life of your Dreams".

Have you ever woken up in the morning with a lack of purpose, direction or focus? Have you ever felt like you're stuck in a rut with no sense of direction? If you answered yes to any of these questions, then don't worry, you're in the right place.

As a qualified Occupational Therapist and Life Coach, I have come across hundreds, if not thousands of people who have felt this very way. The difficulties of life has weighed them down with mental health issues, financial strain and a general sense of hopelessness. The good news is that my experience in coaching these people out of depression, anxiety and hopelessness using the techniques and strategies outlined in this book, helped them regain ground, rebuild their life and increase their sense of well-being, quality of life and satisfaction.

One thing I am very passionate about is helping people to break down mental barriers, achieve their fullest potential and make their dreams a reality. As a pupil of personal development and self-improvement, I have learnt from great thought leaders in the industry on how to take action, take responsibility and build momentum in getting to where you wish to be in life.

The truth is, it is not what happens to you, but life is more about what you will do with what you have been dealt. I hope the information in this book is of service and of value to you. If you would like 1:1 coaching sessions, please contact me at…..

Have a look at the online Lifestyle Redesign Course:

https://temioni.thinkific.com/courses/lifestyle-redesign

Breaking Mental Barriers Podcast Episode with Temi Oni:

https://open.spotify.com/episode/6jgdh4PhjMnEKVxbs56w7A

The Joy of Rejection Podcast Episode with Temi Oni:

https://music.amazon.com/es-cl/podcasts/f5fedad3-0305-45b2-8a7d-8f196f612856/episodes/289f8e4b-875a-4c1f-9a3f-7a8a09ae9ecc/the-happy-joy-the-joy-of-rejection-w-temi-oni

Personal Development Podcast Episode with Temi Oni:

https://open.spotify.com/episode/5X4T84Ylw863mlUijuzPzm

You can check out my YouTube channel here:

https://www.youtube.com/@temicharlotteoni/videos

TESTIMONIALS

"I started the year in a pretty low place, thanks to the pandemic, I'm glad to say I'm ending it on a high, thanks to the lifestyle redesign course" – Anonymous

"Wow, I don't even know what to day. Temi's imaginative way of thinking is amazing. I had been out of a job for many years, battled with mental health issues and felt really stuck in life. The Lifestyle Redesign online course really helped me to get my life together. I've now jot a fab job that I could only have dreamed of and I feel amazing in my mental health. I'm proof that this course works and you should try it." - Anonymous

"The Lifestyle Redesign course I did with Temi was transformative. There was one particular exercise when I imagined myself to be 50 years old and the life I wanted for myself. I am now taking over 2 businesses, something I didn't imagine would be possible. I realised that I valued myself and that I had a position in this world other than the "black sheep" I had identified with. Yes I ruffled some feathers along the way but now I am confident to say that I am securing my financial future and entering into a lifestyle in which I have the means to throw a big party to celebrate my 50th, if I wish. I will no longer need to worry about money in the way I have been for a long time. I will also be my own boss. I can't thank Temi enough for her commitment, inspiration and imaginative way of working both empathetically and not shying away from challenging when appropriate." - Anonymous

"Dealing with stress is something Temi Oni, a Mental Health Practitioner who supports long term unemployed people through Central London Works Work and Health Programme, does on an almost daily basis. But it's her clients who are experiencing stress and its advice and guidance from Temi that has helped hundreds of

people in Central London deal with the issues that are causing them stress.

Telling the story of one of the people she has recently worked with, Temi says: "A client presented with mental health concerns aggravated by current life challenges and struggles - juggling the stresses of being a single parent and supporting their own relatives as well as being out of work. The main challenge this client faced was acknowledging and accepting the need for help, being a person who was used to providing support for others."

Taking time to understand her client and the issues behind her feelings of stress, Temi started to support by listening to what her client was experiencing. "During our initial health support call they were tearful," says Temi, who acknowledges that it is always an amazing feeling to see a client trust who trusts you enough to show their full emotions. After the initial call, Temi worked with her client to help her understand more about the reasons why we experience stress and the impact it can have on our mental and physical health, as well as what her particular concerns were.

Temi continued to support her client through using SMART goals and action planning sessions to plan a way to address the issues that were causing her stress and she also supported client to self-refer to local IAPT psychological services to access help at the right time.

Gradually, the life challenges begun to reduce by working on self-help tools for better self-care.

"On our final appointment, this client presented with bright mood and mentally stability and had recently started applying for Manager roles," says Temi. "They were eager and ready to return back to work. A complete contrast to their initial presentation."

Central London Works health practitioners measure the impact of their support through systems such as PHQ-9, which is a measurement for depression and GAD-7 anxiety disorder measurement. This client indicated a significant reduction in anxiety and depression as well as a PHQ-9 depression score which dropped from 24 to 7 and GAD-7 measurement from 18 to 4 over the 4 months. #Stress Awareness"

- Ingeus

Table of Contents

SELF-DISCOVERY 1
OCCUPATIONAL LIFE AREAS 7
SMART GOALS AND ACTION PLANNING 12
SELF-CARE 20
ADDRESSING NEGATIVE THOUGHT PATTERNS & CYCLES .. 28
POSITIVE SELF-AFFIRMATIONS & BELIEFS 34
RELAXATION SESSION WITH A GUIDED VISUALISATION SESSION 36

CHAPTER 1

SELF-DISCOVERY

Delving deeper into self-discovery

The truth is in life, in order for us to reach our fullest potential, in order for us to get to where we need to be in life, we first have to go deeper into ourselves, to discover who we truly are. Many of us tend to want to get things in the future or in our lives that we first have not yet discovered who we truly are in order for us to obtain those things. Self-discovery is all about finding out who you really are. You might want to ask yourself the question; who am I? When I have done this coaching session with my clients, several of them have define self- discovery as your true potential, your true abilities, to know what you want to do in your life, what makes you feel good? Knowing your purpose in life and sticking to that purpose. Understanding who you really are and discovering more about yourself will reveal where you can potentially go and what you should be potentially doing in life.

When we think about mental health and mental decline, sometimes people feel that there are stuck in a rut or they are unable to push forward in life, because they have not really discovered who they really are yet, or what they should be doing or where they should be going. When I think about those terms, "Stuck in a rut", "confused" "don't know where I'm going", "don't know what I'm working towards." There is a part of us, whether we realise it or not, in our deepest level of being, some might call it the soul or the spirit. But there is a part of the human body, whereby we gain satisfaction, mentally, physically and emotionally by understanding our true identity and by really understanding who we are and also by finding out what our purpose in life actually is. The truth is that true self-discovery is also linked with self-awareness. Self-discovery is the information that we begin to understand about ourselves, but this information is not necessarily obtainable by everybody, it is not even obtainable by ourselves. What do I mean about this? If I was to say that person is a male or that person is a female, I really have not discovered anything about them that is not really a discovery, why? Because anybody could have told you that, true self-discovery is information about ourselves that is not easily obtainable by others or even by ourselves. And so going deeper into who we are and really discovering what we're really about, is a great way to uncover some of the hidden gems and treasures that lies within us. But the truth is that self-discovery should led to self-awareness and what is self-awareness? I've created the equation that self-discovery should lead to self-awareness. Discovery + action = self-awareness. The true essence of self-awareness is not the I am simply aware but that I take an action of what I am aware of. For example, if Chloe understands that she is anxious when she gets around a group of people that she is not familiar with, that is a discovery, that is something that Chloe has discovered about herself. It probably was not always an obtainable piece of information to other people, maybe because Chloe has been able to mask it. But the truth is, Chloe has discovered that she gets anxious when she is around a group of people, especially if it is the first time. The discovery that Chloe has had there, should lead to an action, discovery of self, should lead to an action and the action might be that Chloe is going to work hard on her confidence, maybe she might go to the gym to lose weight, maybe she might read books on personal development, maybe she might meditate or engage in further conversations with people to really improve her social interactions and her discourse. That is an action that Chloe has taken as a result of the discovery and you see, as time goes on Chloe begins to realise that she is becoming more confident in group settings. What is happening there, is that true self-awareness, does not say "ok I am now confident in the group settings, I will now give everything up". True self- awareness is that I understand the tendency for myself to be anxious in this situation is still there, however, if I don't work on it or continue to work on it through personal development or self-improvement, then I am likely to become anxious again in future. So although Chloe might feel confident today, it is as a result of the action that she has put behind the self-discovery. I believe that true self-discovery is when discovery of self + an action, is what really leads to self-awareness. You can't claim that you're truly self-aware, until you have actually put an action behind it, because without an action you are still in the phase of self-discovery. You see at the level of self- discovery there really is not much responsibility. For example, Chloe finds out that she is anxious in that setting, she might not be response at that level, which is level 1 of the discovery. Discovery is the lower level, is the least, in terms of growth. If I discover something about myself, I am not yet responsible, but you see once we go to the next step, I now become responsible once I put an action behind what I have discovered – because I can no longer claim that I am not aware. Discovery is being somewhat aware of yourself, but self-awareness is putting an action behind what you have discovered. From here, there are higher levels [i.e. self-discovery, self-awareness and self-mastery] and all of these different levels that we can achieve when we really tap into who we really are, when we really embrace and think about how can we grow and what areas of ourselves have we not tapped into and discovered, we begin to realise there is so much treasure inside of us that we had probably not realised.

So I am going to leave you with a motivational piece of content. This is an acronym that I created myself and I have shared it with people on podcasts and coaching sessions. It has been a really impactful and helpful acronym.

It's the WVP – WVP has been an acronym that I have coined and it has really helped me in my life and in my journey of staying aligned to my purpose and where I want to be in my life.

The W stands for MY WHY – Why am I starting a new business? Why do I want to become successful for example? For some people, the answer to these questions might be that they want to create a beautiful life for themselves and their family. For others it might be that they just want to become financially independent. The truth is, understanding your why, understanding the reason that you are doing whatever it is that you are doing, is a part of your self-discovery journey. Because we know that life is about ups and downs, one thing we are guaranteed will be challenges and obstacles, but the truth is understanding your why, the reason and the purpose for what you are doing and the reason for what it is that you want, will help you when the storms of life comes, when the obstacles arise and when the hurdles are present. Know your why.

The V stands for MY VALUE – I believe every single human being that will walk the face of the Earth has intrinsic value.

That means that by just literally existing on the surface of the Earth, even if you didn't go to university or have education or all of these different training. We are all born with innate gifts, skills and abilities, we have experiences, we have things that we can show up and serve the world with. So you might want to sit with yourself for a moment and think "What are the skills that I have? What are the services that I have? What are the experiences that I have been through? How can I show up and serve other people with these innate gifting's and abilities that I have? What problems can I solve? What questions can I answer? How can I be of service to other people?

The P stands for MY PURPOSE – you see, you might want to ask yourself questions in relation to your purpose such as "why was I born?" "What is the reason I came here?" "What is my legacy?" "How do I want to show up in the world?" "How do I want to be remembered?" Always remember that these questions are not just questions that we put any answer to and tick off. These are the sorts of questions that you might just want to sit and chew on and ponder, and that's ok. Because the truth is, I see the WVP acronym as a framework. You see, in 5 years' time you could still ask yourself the same questions to see if you're aligned in your life, if you're going in the right direction. I like to see it as a framework as a structure, as a way to frame your life and see "am I within the right parameters that I should be living in?" You see in life, there is really no right or wrong when it comes to the answers to some of these questions. But the truth is, if we never ask ourselves these questions, we never dig a bit deeper into who we really are and where we are going.

We've gone through a lot of content and the chapter will be coming to an end very soon. Before we end it, we are going to do a visualization session. We are going to visualise our 80 or 90 year old self, I want you to close your eyes, I want you to remove all distractions and I want you to sit in a quiet place right now. And when you are closing your eyes, I want you to remove all your thoughts, all the racing thoughts going through your mind in this moment. As you are closing your eyes, I want you to envision, your 80 or 90 year old self staring back at you, what does he or she look like? Do they have any wrinkles on their face? Is there any grey hair? Are they smiling? Are they frowning? Are they happy? Are they sad? And the reason why I want you to just sit with that image of your 80 or 90 year old self, is because I want you to realise everything that you are doing in your life today, the decisions that you are making, the choices that you take, the path that you go on – is all directly impacting that 80 or 90 year old self. And it helps us to realise that we need to be more intentional with the way that we live our lives, that we need to understand that that person looking back at you right now, you are responsible for them, their happiness, their health, their success, that's all in your hands today. You see when we are younger, we tend to think we have a lot of time, we think that time is actually in our hands, but the truth is, it is not. In the blink of an eye, it can all go and we can either make the right decisions or the wrong ones, and that will impact our 80 or 90 year old self. Our decisions, whether we choose to live at a higher level of understanding, of self-awareness, of self- discovery and potentially reach self-mastery is actually within our grasp. It would be amazing to know that you did the best that you could and that you pleased your 80 and 90 year old self. You can open your eyes now, we have ended this chapter. This is the end of the chapter, where we have has a taster of self-discovery. Please note that at the end of this chapter, there will be course notes and homework, so if you ever want to go back, review, ponder or answer any of the questions, you're welcome to. When you feel ready, let's go into chapter 2.

CHAPTER 2

OCCUPATIONAL LIFE AREAS

Reviewing our occupational life areas

In session 2, we're going to be looking at the different occupational life areas. As an Occupational Therapist, I work with people day in and day out, to look and assess their life as see where their own lifestyle might actually be bringing distress, dissatisfaction and sorrow to their own experience in life. The truth is, when we think about life, we have been brought up a certain way, or we have experienced life a certain way or we have lived life a certain way and we don't realise that we have the opportunity, the ability to actually start redesigning how we are living. It would literally be insanity, to be doing the same thing over and over again and then expect a whole new result. Insanity right? But the truth is, when I have spoken with people in coaching sessions, in 1:1 sessions, we've had valuable content, we have had valuable discourse about what was bringing them down and what was making them feel sad. At the heart of their narration, when I was listening to what they were saying, is that mentally they felt so sad with how they were experiencing their own life. The thing is, sometimes we don't realise that the answer might be within our own grasp, within our own hands and within our own reach. So what are occupational life areas?

Occupational life areas are the various areas in our lives that bring us satisfaction, meaning, wholeness and also balance to our lives. There is a certain thing called occupational balance, which means, how balanced am I in the various areas of my life. You see, if someone was always working at set goals that were just about work, that person might be improving or excelling in their work, but all the other areas of their life, maybe their health, nutrition, leisure time and their social life might all be impacted negatively as a result of this imbalance. And you see, when we feel imbalanced in our lives, it tends to bring mental dissatisfaction. So we can actually bring to reserve these feelings of mental dissatisfaction by simply redesigning how we're living our lives. By simply tapping into various occupations that will boost our mental health, our state of living, and our state of life. We know for example the first areas being physical exercise and activity. It is so easy to neglect exercise and physical activity. I know for myself, for many year before, I didn't really engage too much in exercise. When I studied to become an Occupational Therapist on my Master's course, I really engaged in running. Seriously, going running, and I saw the impact, the value that running brought to my life and to my mental health. It was a way for me to distress, it was a way for me to mind- set train, it was a way for me to develop my endurance, mentally, emotionally, physically. It was a way for me to be disciplined, it was also a way for me to lose weight. I really a very important principle, the fact that everything effects everything. You see, when I was going for my morning run, I would come back and I would eat healthily, because everything effects everything. And because I had gone for a run and eaten healthily, I would sit down at work and I would have a better presentation and a more effective day. And I wondered, what is it that is going on here, why is it that from one occupation, I have engaged in in the morning. Why is it bleeding throughout the day? And positively impacting the rest of my occupational life areas? And then I was ending the way feeling so satisfied and wanting to repeat this again. Well, this is the importance of occupational life areas and thinking about what we are engaging in and how we are engaging in it, and how this is impacting the rest of our life and the rest of our areas in life. The second is obviously healthy eating and nutrition. We know that what we put into our bodies is so important for how we feel. The next area being personal care, hygiene, sleep and self-care. The truth is self-care is very important and when I have spoken with people in sessions that might feel that they have had depression, or feel low in mood or have anxiety, sometimes some of these areas become neglected. So we have to be even more mindful of this and be even more aware of this so that we don't neglect any occupational life areas.

The next area is what we call creative expressions of self, and you see, it is so important that we make time to actually express ourselves. For some people, it might be music and signing, for other people, it might be painting, drawing, art – there is a sense of wellbeing and satisfaction when we engage in an outlet that allows us to express ourselves in a creative art format. Some people, it could be playing the piano, it could be creating a song. All of these various activities that boost mental health and give us a greater sense of quality of living and satisfaction.

The next are is work and productivity. The two are similar, but not the same. Work is obviously very essential for mental health and general sense of well-being. We know from research that people who are employed tend to experience higher levels of mental health satisfaction, compared to their unemployed counterparts. This is research from people who do not necessarily love their job. That shows you that employment and work is so important for mental health and wellbeing. There is a part of each and every one of us that we need to feel that we have overcome challenges, that we have utilised our skillset, that we have put to use and been productive in the day. Although work and productivity are similar, they are not the same. Why do I say that? You see, I worked on a project with a lot of unemployed people, who experienced mental health decline or deterioration. Obviously, they were not working, but I coached them to make sure that whilst they were working towards getting a job, they remained productive in their days. Guess what I found? Although they were not working in a job yet, because we had set a plan to be productive in their days, they came out of that week feeling higher in their mental health and wellbeing. Feeling more productive, useful and feeling like they have actually accomplished something. And so that is important, whether we are employed or we work for ourselves, whether we are unemployed, we must stay productive. True productivity is when we are able to create a product out of the activities and the actions that we have engaged in throughout the day.

The next area is fun and leisure and Oh my, isn't this important? We need to schedule in fun and leisure just like we schedule in our work commitments. Fun and leisure is essential, work hard, play hard, it's just as important.

The last area is social interaction, social interaction is so important that's how we develop our social skills. That's how we learn from other people, that's how we understand other people's cultural backgrounds, experiences, abilities and we are able to rub minds with like-minded people. Social interaction is important. But you see all of these areas that we have looked into [i.e. physical exercise, healthy eating, personal care, creative expressions of self, work and productivity, fun and leisure, social interaction], if we neglect any of these areas, we will tend to feel it in our overall sense of wellbeing and mental state.

So, we are coming to the end of session 2, and I want you to ponder on these few questions.

Which areas of your life have you neglected and why? How can you cater for this neglect?

It's so essential that we really improve our quality of life by taking stock of how we live our lives, of being more intentional of the things that we engage in throughout the day and make sure that we are engaging in meaningful activities and occupations.

Well, we have come to the end of session2, I will see you in session 3, let's go...

CHAPTER 3

SMART GOALS AND ACTION PLANNING

Creating your dream life through SMART and strategic goals!

In session 3, we are going to be reviewing the topic of SMART goals and action planning. SMART goals are so essential, when we think about redesigning our lives. If we are not setting goals that are SMART, then we are essentially setting ourselves up to fail. It is important that we set goals that are specific, measurable, attainable, realistic and timely. And you see there is a whole action plan as to how we can navigate the goal setting process and we're going to go through those steps. But before we do, I want you to think really holistically when setting your goals. In chapter 2, we just reviewed the different occupational life areas, and so really when we're setting goals, we need to make sure that we have a goal in at least in one of those occupational life areas to feel more balanced, whole and to make sure that your life is growing evenly instead of just in one area. Let's start the action planning process.

STEP 1 – identify the goal.

How do we know what it is that we're hoping to achieve, if we don't even think about identifying what it is that we want to achieve? You see many of us, we know that we want to have a different life or a different experience. Or we want to achieve goals or we want to have a great future, but we don't set a goal. So we're hoping and we're wishing but nothing is actually set in place, and nothing is actually being defined. Goals are essential, I always see goals as a vehicle to your destiny, I don't think goals are an end in and of itself, but it is almost like a means to an end. You set a goal to accomplish a certain outcome or objective. You set a goal to be at a certain objective or outcome by a certain age for example. So goals in my mind are more of an avenue and more of a vehicle to getting to where you hope to be in the future. So as I said before, step 1 is about identifying the goal. It is important that you break your goals down, so that they are not overwhelming. We know that if we set goals that are too extreme, we are more likely to fail and we are more likely to feel overwhelmed and low in mood and then not likely to get back up and keep going with it. We need to make sure that we are setting ourselves up to succeed, and not setting ourselves up to fail. This is why we're going to make goals that our specific, measurable, achievable, realistic and timely.

STEP 2 – Use a prompt if required.

This step can mean two things, the first is that if we have a goal, we can use visual prompts [i.e. a wall planner] this might be really helpful for people who are visualise learners to have a visual prompt in front of you and to literally put down all of the goals that you need to accomplish in the month or in the day. Have it all written down so that it is not in your mind, but rather it is on the page, and it is therefore you to see every day, every morning or in the evening, you're able to see what is is that you need to do. This helps to ensure things do not feel so overwhelming, when we have written down our goals in our diaries or wall planner we tend to feel a lot more in control. We tend to feel like it is more manageable, we can see it, we know what we're meant to be doing each day. So it can be really helpful in processing what it is that we have to do. A lot of us tend to keep our goals in our minds, we get overwhelmed by that, and then we do not actually accomplish it, because we're so overwhelmed. But to help ourselves, to help our brains, to really chunk down all the information and transfer it into bite size information of what we need to do, we need to use prompts. Prompts could be to do lists, a wall planner, sticky note pads – all the things that help us to break down those goals so they're not overwhelming is essential.

The second element of this step, is also about thinking about areas within a certain goal that you specifically need to work on. What do I mean by this? Let's say your overarching goal is to get a fantastic job in the centre of London. Well – maybe you're really good with all the parts that comes with getting a job, but the element that you really need to work on when you think about your goal for this one is the aspect of interviews. Maybe that is an area whereby you're not that good, maybe you're great with writing your CV, and you're great with writing your applications, but perhaps it is specifically the interview that you need to focus on. Well – you can use your visual aids or prompts and you can think about areas of the interview that you need to work on. This could be how you present yourself in terms of how you speak, how you sell yourself and your skills, experiences and expertise in the interview. This might be how you dress or how you groom yourself, this might be how you're able to kind of keep your nerves in check. All of these things are about honing into a specific element in the goal, using the prompts and focusing and honing in on the weak parts, so that you're more likely to achieve your goal.

STEP 3 – Think about the how

One thing that is important to remember, is that the goal setting process is a very reflective and dynamic process. What do I mean by this? Well – when we think about how we're going to achieve something that we want to set out to do, the how, helps us to think about how we are actually going to do it right? So when we think about it, it is a very reflective process, maybe the how might change in 2 weeks. Maybe the how is not working for today and will need to be reviewed later on. So the how? Is a question that we need to ask ourselves? And we might also ask ourselves in this same step, things such as, how will you know when you have achieved the goal? What will you need to do before you have achieved this goal? Where can you get help if you need it? What will you gain by doing this? What will you lose? What will you do once you have achieved this goal? So these questions are all about the how, it's all about the process. It's all about the strategy of how you're going to accomplish your goals. You might want to document your answers to these questions and keep a copy of it in a file. It might help you to think about how it is going, especially if it is a long-term goal. Maybe you're thinking about buying your first time property that might be more of a longer term goal. Maybe you're hoping to write your first book. I don't know what they goal might be, but maybe thinking about the how, especially if it is a very long-term goal or it is going to take a bit of time to accomplish it, it might be really helpful to document some of the answers to these questions.

STEP 4 – Thinking about using a 4 week planner

I have already spoken about using a visual aid, like a wall chart or a planner. It's so essential – and why do I say this? Let's take for example, Chloe wants to lost 20lbs in 4 weeks. Chloe has to think about all the small little tasks that she has to complete in order to come out of that month, 20lbs lighter. What might this look like? She might have to think about the food that she is going to eat, what sort of meals is she going to do? Is she going to do a meal prep? When is she going to do the shopping? Is she going to do it on the weekend? When is it going to be done? She might also need to think about how many times is she going to exercise? Is it going to be 3x per week or 4? What exercise is it going to be? Will it be running or will it be yoga? She might also think about how many times will she be weighing in? Or will she weight herself in that time? Will it be once a week or will it be every day? Will it be once at the end of the month? What will that look like? And so all the answers to these questions, will need to be put into the 4 week planner. This is how we're able to see how Chloe is going to come out of the month 20lbs lighter. This helps to break down that feeling of being overwhelmed by quite a big goal.

STEP 5 – Regularly review

I previously mentioned that the goal planning and setting process is a dynamic and a reflective process. Things are always changing and so there is always a lot more that we can reflect on. So how do we know that we have even achieved a goal, if we don't sit back to review how it's actually gone? Things that you might want to ask yourself within this step are, what have you achieved this week? What's gone well? What difficulties have you faced? How could you have overcome these difficulties if you had any? What if anything has stopped you achieving what you set out to? What support do you need to achieve next week's actions? Understanding how the process of goal setting is going and being reflective on it, is so important for monitoring your success and progress in achieving your goal.

STEP 6 – What's next?

So now we're at the end of the month and let's say Chloe has come out 20lbs lighter in her weight. Let's say she crushed it, and she was able to stick with her goal – fantastic! Well, she might want to think about looking at other occupational life areas. Maybe she has ticked off the physical exercise area, and she might want to look into another occupational life area to avoid neglecting any other area.

But let's say she came out of the month and was not able to achieve her goal of coming out 20lbs lighter in her weight. Well we might want to think about why that is. Maybe a month was too long for Chloe and maybe a 2 week action plan would have been more appropriate. It is important to note that some people find it quite difficult to set goals that are quite long in duration. Some people do really well with shorter time frames in terms of their action plan. And that's fine, no one way is right or wrong. It is about understanding how you best operate and working towards that. The next thing Chloe might want to think about is maybe the goal has changed due to barriers and circumstances. We know that life is changing rapidly, we know that things happen very quickly and maybe their have been changes in Chloe's life that meant that her goal has been impacted. It's all about staying reflective and thinking about what caused a barrier for Chloe to achieve the goal. What circumstances arose that meant that she was delayed or stopped in achieving that goal. It's about asking those questions so that you know the answer, and you know how to get back on track and continue forward with the goal.

Another thing Chloe might want to consider is maybe the actions that she set just were not realistic and that is what hindered the achievement of the action plan. Let's say that Chloe was going to lose 20-50lbs in one day, we know that that would not have been realistic, nor would it have even been healthy. So sometimes when we're setting goals, it is important that we're not being overly zealous or overly ambitious, that we are not actually just setting ourselves up to fail. We need to make sure our goals embody the acronym of specific, measurable, achievable, realistic and timely – for us to really be able to go ahead and achieve it.

We're coming to the end of chapter 3 and before we end, here is a homework.

This homework is about thinking about 5 SMART goals, I want you to use the paper that is attached on the following page.

Write down 5 SMART goals that cover a variety of different occupational life areas. An example might be that Suzanne has decided for her first goal, it will be physical exercise.

So she might write,

Suzanne is to spend 30 minutes every morning, 4x a week going for a morning run before she starts her work.

It's quite specific because we know when she is going to be doing it [i.e. in the morning], we know how long she is going to be doing it for [i.e. 30 minutes] and we know what she is going to be doing [i.e. running]. So if you can think about 5 SMART goals that you're going to put down this week, that cover the different occupational life areas that we covered in chapter 2, then go ahead and set your 5 SMART goals. And remember, the more balanced you can be in your life when you're setting your goals, the more sense of satisfaction and general quality of life, you will experience. We have come to the end of chapter 3, I can't wait for you to join me again in chapter 4!

CHAPTER 4

SELF-CARE

Session 4 – Learning to look after yourself properly.

We're going to look into the topic of self-care and also self-love, and why this is so important in our lifestyle redesign. When I have spoken with clients in coaching sessions, they have defined self-care as putting yourself first, looking after yourself, not just putting other people first, but also prioritising yourself. It's kind of like a life battery, ensuring you're fully charged otherwise if you're not you might have a breakdown and stop functionally optimally. Someone else said "it's about looking after the whole person, including the emotional", someone else said "it's about loving themselves, knowing their value and sticking to it." Someone else said, "It's about taking time out for yourself, concentrating on yourself, looking after yourself mentally and physically."

The topic of self-care, is a topic that is close to my heart, and it's one that I really started to embrace in my own life. It's also a topic that I have coached several people about in 1:1 coaching sessions. The topic of self-care, is such a deep and emotional topic that when we truly understand it in its really raw form, we're about to start embracing this concept and really take it on. And thereby, change our life and our experiences and the way that we see and process life, as well as the way that we perceive the things around us.

What is self-care? If we take for example, the analogy of a cup, self- care can be likened to this. You see, if we think about a cup, we have all the things coming into the cup and we have all the things going out of the cup. The things coming out of the cup could be negative people, difficult situations and circumstances, it could be health challenges and illnesses. These are all the things that drain our cup right? But then we have the things that go into our cups, this could be meditation, prayer, positive people, personal development, exercising, health eating – these are all the things that help us to fill the proverbial cup right? I believe that true self-care is not about being selfish. Self-care is about looking after oneself, so that you can actually be of value and of service to other people. You see we cannot give what we first have not obtained for ourselves. If I have not poured into myself, I have nothing to pour into somebody else. And so if we return back to the analogy of the cup, self-care is about acknowledging that things are coming out of my cup. And what are these things that are coming out of my cup? But it is also about acknowledging that I have the responsibility of maintaining what is coming out of my cup by pouring back into my cup. You see, if we think about self-care, we can think about it in the analogy of a plane right? In the case of an emergency, you have to put your own oxygen mask on before that of anyone else, even that of an infant – isn't that horrible? Well, no, because in order to help someone else, you must first have helped yourself. In order to pour out into someone else, you must first have poured back into yourself. The truth is, you cannot give what you have not first obtained. When you think about the cup, a lot of people tend to burnout, and that is when the cup is completely empty. At this point, there is nothing to give, there is nothing to be able to pour back into other people. That's when our emotions, our mental state and even our physical state can be at an all-time low. So how can we manage the cup so that we do not get to a place where it is very difficult to be able to fill the cup back up to the brim again? Well, we're going to look into what self-care really is, and we're going to address what I have coined at the 4 quadrants of self-care activities.

Self-care activities are those things we engage in that provide nourishment, revitalisation and enrichment to both ourselves and our lives. I've coined the phrase, the 4 quadrants of self-care activities, because it helped me to explain to the clients that I was coaching, the areas of responsibilities and awareness that we need to be mindful of when thinking about our self-care.

The first quadrant – PHYSICAL

Now this could be about the pamper days, spa days, going for a facial, physical exercise, health eating, skin routines and all the things we do to care for our physical bodies. This is great, but the problem is, a lot of us tend to think that this is the entirety of self-care. Especially on social media, a lot of people are all about the spa and pampering but that is just literally touching the brim of self-care. Self-care is much deeper than that, and we're going to see that as we keep going.

The second quadrant – MENTAL

So this is about, acknowledging that we have a duty to care for ourselves from a mental health perspective. The activities within this category might look like meditation, prayer, journaling, writing and personal development. When we exercise the mind, explore other avenues and stretch our mind by reading, personal development and journaling; we're able to stretch our minds to be more open, aware, to question etc. - that's a great way to also develop, grow and care for ourselves mentally.

The third quadrant – EMOTIONAL

You might be thinking, do I need to care for myself from an emotional standpoint? But of course, we do. Activities that we can do and engage in that is going to help us to care for ourselves emotionally, might be helping others. You might be thinking, should I really be helping other people so that I can just feel good about myself? But the truth is, whether we realise it or not, there is a part of every human being that by just doing good to other people, we actually feel better about ourselves from an emotional standpoint. When we put ourselves aside, and we choose to focus on other people's problems, that this might look like feeding the homeless, giving to charity, mentoring and coaching other people through difficult circumstances that you have been able to overcome. There is a sense that we tend to feel good from an emotional standpoint.

The final quadrant – SOCIAL

You see, we have a duty to care for ourselves from a social perspective as well. If we allow the wrong people into our lives from the social quadrant, they are probably going to undo all the other areas of the quadrant. You allow one toxic person in from the social quadrant, and they will probably undo the emotional, mental and maybe even the physical. So we have a duty to make sure that we are spending time, with quality people who enrich our lives, make us feel happier and make us feel that we are valued. That becomes our responsibility.

Before we go onto the next segment of this chapter, I just want you to think about these 4 areas and think about our life. Have you been aware of these 4 areas? Are there things that you need to do to change or is everything okay? I'll give you a moment to think about that…

Now moving into the second section of this chapter, we're going to be looking into self-love. Why? Haven't we just reviewed the topic of self-care and aren't they the same thing? No – of course not, self-care is how we care for ourselves. But the truth is, how can we care for ourselves, if you have not actually begun to really love yourself from a self-love perspective.

I've also asked people that I have coached before, what they think their definition of self-love is, and some of them said, "It's about being kind to yourself, recognising that you wouldn't speak to other people the way that you speak to yourself." "Being gentle and kind to yourself" "Acknowledging the good things about yourself including the flaws", someone else said it is about "kindness and compassion" someone else said it is about "getting to know themselves and what makes them feel comfortable and not just shoving things under the carpet." Someone said it is about "accepting herself and who she is and her journey." Someone else defined it as "knowing their value and accepting it, making sure that they stand firm in who he is, meditating and speaking life in himself and getting to know himself each day." Well these are other people's definition of self-love and I want you to think about what self-love means to you.

Self-love is not about thinking that you are the best thing since slice bread, self-love is not arrogance or thinking that you have no flaws. Actually true self-love is that I acknowledge that I have strengths and that I have weaknesses, but I am accepting of both states and of both parts of myself. To really love yourself, you must be able to accept the good and the not so good about yourself. Of course, once you have accepted the not so good, you can always work on those areas through personal development and self-improvement. But it's about being aware that you're not just completely good, there are strengths and there are weaknesses, but you are accepting of both parts and both states of yourself.

We're going to go into the 5 self-love languages. You might have heard of this phrase before, you know the love languages? The truth is, we tend to think about love languages when we're in a couple, or when we're thinking about our partner, but it's really important for us to understand our own love language before we get into a couple, or before we think about someone else. How can you love someone else, when you don't even know how to love yourself or you don't understand how you receive love? Let's go through the 5 self-love languages.

The first one is words of affirmation – people within this category need to self-affirm their positive beliefs about themselves. They might want to build up a personal journal routine and write down positive self-affirmations and beliefs about themselves.

The second one is physical touch – people within this category need to discover what makes them feel good physically and this could be from treating themselves to a luxury massage in a spa, or treating themselves to a self-pampering routine at home, caring for your body, is a perfect way to show yourself love, especially if that is your personal self-love language.

The third one is receiving gifts – people within this category need to treat themselves to a spa date or maybe something that they have always wanted for a really long time, if that is obviously your self- love language.

The fourth one is acts of service – people within this category need to do things daily that help them feel more organised, this will increase their wellbeing and make them feel more at peace.

The last one is quality time and solitude – people within this category, must set aside personal time for themselves, to do something nourishing and relaxing. This could be yoga, journaling, walking or even reading a book.

These are the 5 self-love languages and you see it is important to note that many people tend to fall in about 2-3 of these self-love languages. It's important to note that you might actually have more than one self- love language and that's okay. But understanding how you receive love, is so important in your lifestyle redesign. Always remember, that in order for you to obtain what you want in life, in order for you to get to where you need to be in life and to achieve your fullest potential – you must think about what is coming out of my cup and what is going into my cup. Once you are aware of this, it's then important to schedule in a self-care time, just as you would your work commitments, your appointments in your diary, you would need to also diary in your self-care time. This might look like, once a month or twice a week, three times a fortnight? I can't set that for you, that's part of your journey and it's for you to accomplish that for yourself.

We're coming towards the end of chapter 4, and before we end I want you to complete the homework found on the next page.

Think about the areas of your life, which you may have neglected in the last 2 weeks.

Create a plan to address these key areas. It might be that you start off with "over the next 2 weeks I will…"

I hope you have enjoyed chapter 4, I hope it has been of service and of value to you. I will see you over in chapter 5!

CHAPTER 5

ADDRESSING NEGATIVE THOUGHT PATTERNS & CYCLES

Replacing negative thoughts with more positive and helpful thinking styles

If we want to get to where we want to be in life, we really need to change the way that we think. Could your own mind-set and your own thoughts, be stopping you from getting to where you need to be in life? If that is the case, there is no need to worry – we're going to address how to really change negative thinking patterns. You see most of us spend a lot of time in our own minds, worrying about the future, replaying events of the past and generally focusing on things that leave us feeling dissatisfied, upset, low, confused and you see this is a very common thing. We as humans, tends to focus more on the negative than the positive. But the truth is, focusing more on negative thinking, will actually leave you distracted, and will actually drain your energy and can make you feel more anxious and/or depressed.

But it is not all doom and gloom of course, this book's purpose is to help you redesign your life. The good news is, that with dedicated practice you can actually replace negative thinking patterns with thoughts that can actually help you redesign your life. This can obviously make a huge difference and a huge impact to your day to day quality of life, happiness and satisfaction.

The first way we can start challenging these negative thinking patterns and habits that come into our lives, is to recognise thought distortions. Our minds have a really clever way of convincing us of something that just simply isn't true. These things can look like they're true, although they're not. That's what a distortion is after all. But if we can recognise these distortions, we can then learn to challenge them. We're going to go through the more common thought distortions that people tend to have.

The first one is black and white thinking; this is when we see everything through the filter of everything literally being black and white. It's either one way or another, there is no grey area in between and this can lead to negative thinking.

The second one is personalising, this is assuming that you are to blame for anything that goes wrong. This is assuming that you are to blame for someone who didn't smile at you as you're walking across the street and you're assuming that it's because you did something wrong. Now wouldn't that be crazy to assume that you did something wrong, because a stranger is frowning at you on the street. Perhaps they just had a bad day, maybe they left their home arguing with their relative, or maybe it's just not going well for them right now. But personalising is when we personalise someone else's emotions or expressions and we attribute that to us.

The third one is filter thinking, which is choosing to see only the negative side of a situation. We know that life is never just bad, there are positives as well, but if you choose just to focus and see the negative that can also lead to perpetuating negative thought patterns and cycles.

The fourth one is catastrophising, which is assuming that the worst possible outcome is going to happen. I'm sure we have all done this one right? Before we get to the interview we're already assuming that it is going to go badly and we're going to get so anxious and nervous before we have even sat down or reached the venue, we're already catastrophising. This can lead to negative thought patterns and cycles. But the good thing is we can challenge negative thinking. Whenever we have a distorted thought, we do need to stop and evaluate whether it is actually do. Did the person that walked out of their own home and I met them on the street, are they frowning at me because I did something wrong? Would that be logical? We would need to stop and evaluate that thought. The moment we begin to stop and evaluate the thought, we begin to realise that it cannot be logical for that to be related to me, because I have no correlation to the person and they have no correlation to me. Therefore, it is very unlikely that their frowning is as a result of me. You see, we have to think about how we respond to our friends when they put themselves down. If your friend called Samantha, was always putting herself down, I'm sure you would probably offer a good rebuttal or a good reason to see things from a positive state of mind. We have to apply this same logic to ourselves, we have to become that best friend to ourselves internally. I always tell the people that I coach, what is the state of your internal environment? Ask yourself, are you assuming the worst that will happen? Are you blaming yourself for something that has not gone the way you wanted? Think about other possible outcomes or reasons that something has turned out differently than you hoped. Another way to challenge these negative thought cycles is to take a break from negative thinking. You might be thinking how? But the truth is, it is possible, we can learn to separate ourselves from negative thoughts. Most people tend to think, they just have to think positive or have a positive state of mind. To some extent that is true, but actually a good way that you can take a break from negative thinking, is to actually allow yourself to entertain the thought for a small amount of time. Recurring thoughts tend to reoccur because we tend to brush the thought away, rather than process the thought, evaluate it and spend time with the actual thought. Once we spend time on the thought, once we process the thought, once we evaluate the thought, we begin to realise the fact that the thought is distorted, it's illogical and we're more likely to discharge the thought. Once we have discharged the thought, we've processed it and evaluated it, it's less likely that we're going to return back to that thought.

Another way to start challenging our negative thinking habits, is by realising the judgment. We all judge ourselves and we all judge other people, whether consciously or unconsciously. We're always constantly comparing ourselves and our lives to other people and this will breed dissatisfaction. When you are able to let go of the judgement, you're more likely to feel at ease. Some ways to take a break from judgmental thoughts, might include recognising your own reactions, observing and letting it go. I love the technique of positively judging, this is when you notice that you are negatively judging a person, yourself or a situation – you have to look for a positive quality too. Life is never just negative and when we think about judgment, it always have a negative connotation. Judgment is actually a neutral term and it's about whether we are judging positively or negatively.

One way that we can get out of this perpetual cycle of negative thoughts is to literally positively judge others.

The next way that we can challenge negative thinking, is by practising gratitude. We know that there is so much that we have to be grateful for, no matter how little or how much you have. No matter what you have been through, there is a part of every one of us that we have to be grateful, because everyone has something to be grateful for. Research shows that being grateful has a big impact on your levels of positivity and happiness. Even when you are experiencing a challenging time in your life, you can usually find things to be grateful for, even small things. Noticing the things that are going well and making you feel happy, will keep you more in touch with them. Of course, keeping a gratitude journal and writing things down in it every day, is a great and effective way for remaining grateful and staying positive.

Another way we can start challenging these perpetual negative thinking habits, is by focusing on our strengths. As I previously mentioned, it is human nature to tend to dwell on the negative and overlook the positive. You could have 100 people telling you how fantastic you are at a certain skill or ability, but it only takes 1 or 2 people to say or do something contrary or negative, and you're zooming in on their comments and ignoring the hundreds of other people who have left positive comments. This is human nature, but you see the more you can practice on focusing on your strengths and not dwelling on the mistakes you have made; the easier it will be to feel positive about yourself and also the direction that your life is taking. If you find yourself thinking harsh thoughts about your personality or your actions, take a moment, to stop and think about something that you actually like about yourself.

The last one, is that we can actually start challenging negative thinking, by just seeking out professional support. If you feel that you are struggling to actually manage your thinking habits and you find that they are really interfering with your daily responsibilities or ability to enjoy life, of course there are counselling support and therapeutic intervention to help you weather the life changes, reduce the emotional suffering and experience self-growth, which can ultimately lead to your lifestyle redesign.

We're about to end chapter 5, but before we do, here's a homework.

I want you to think about 5 strengths that you have and write them down and 5 things that you like about yourself and write them down.

Think about 5 things that you have achieved and you are proud of and write them down.

We've come to the end of addressing negative thought patterns and cycles, I hope this chapter has been of value and of service to you and I will see you in chapter 6.

CHAPTER 6

POSITIVE SELF-AFFIRMATIONS & BELIEFS

Affirming our own positive beliefs

It's so important that we self-affirm who we are, are strengths our abilities and our beliefs about ourselves. As this will help us to further increase our sense of identity and self-awareness about who we really are. In coaching sessions with my clients, I've always encouraged them to write down 5 powerful meaningful positive self-affirmations as stick them around their home, in places you visit every day [i.e. mirror, fridge, bedroom etc.]. This is so that you can see these affirmations and it just becomes a natural state of thought. A large part of lifestyle redesign and changing our life experiences is also linked to the change of mind-set and how we perceive ourselves, as well as those around us. Positive self-affirmations are a fantastic way, to start putting on a mental scaffolding or framework, whereby we can start thinking more positively about ourselves and our abilities. In this chapter, is going to be a very short one, and the ball is more in your court.

I want you to write down 5 personal and powerful positive self-affirmations. Please note that your self-affirmations should not be easily copied by another person. Someone else should not be able to come into your home, and take your positive self-affirmations and stick it on their fridge. It needs to be so personal, that it is literally about you. I always tell people that you could write down actual phrases, perhaps you had a past manager who said "you're so fanstic with giving presentation" or maybe you have had a family member who said they were "so proud of you" or perhaps you helped someone and they affirmed you. If you can think back, to a point in your life, whereby people have actually made real statements and comments about you, then write them down. I think it is more powerful and more emotive when self-affirmations are really positive statements that have come from people who have self-affirmed you in your past. I personally think that the generic positive self-affirmations [i.e. "I am strong or I am confident"], those ones are good, but I find that sometimes with the clients that I have worked with, they haven't really worked that well, because they are so generic and it is very easily to not believe them. Therefore, try and make your self- affirmations quite personal, meaningful, emotive and powerful and stick them around your home in places that you frequent all the time. You might want to out one on the window or the mirror.

I will leave you with that task and I will see you in the last chapter, chapter 7. I will see you over there.

CHAPTER 7

RELAXATION SESSION WITH A GUIDED VISUALISATION SESSION

Welcome to the final chapter, in this chapter, we will be doing a relaxation and a guided visualisation session. Play some soothing music and get someone else to read the script below to you.

Visualization relaxation is an effective way to relax the mind and body by picturing a relaxing scene, such as a beach, garden, meadow, or any other peaceful place.

This beach visualization script guides you to relax by imagining spending time on a beautiful beach.

You can use this relaxation script to record your own audio or learn to relax.

Get comfortable. Sit in a supportive chair or lie on your back.

Relax your body by releasing any areas of tension. Allow your arms to go limp... then your legs....

Feel your arms and legs becoming loose and relaxed...

Now relax your neck and back by relaxing your spine.... release the hold of your muscles all the way from your head, down your neck....along each vertebra to the tip of your spine...

Breathe deeply into your diaphragm, drawing air fully into your lungs.... and release the air with a whooshing sound....

Breathe in again, slowly.... pause for a moment.... and breathe out..... Draw a deep breath in.... and out....

In..... Out.....

Become more and more relaxed with each breath....

Feel your body giving up all the tension.... becoming relaxed.... and calm.... peaceful....

Feel a wave of relaxation flow from the soles of your feet, to your ankles, lower legs, hips, pelvic area, abdomen, chest, back, hands, lower arms, elbows, upper arms, shoulders, neck, back of your head, face, and the top of your head....

Allow your entire body to rest heavily on the surface where you sit or lie. Now that your body is fully relaxed, allow the visualization relaxation to begin.

Imagine you are walking toward the ocean.... walking through a beautiful, tropical forest....

You can hear the waves up ahead.... you can smell the ocean spray.... the air is moist and warm.... feel a pleasant, cool breeze blowing through the trees....

You walk along a path....coming closer to the sea....as you come to the edge of the trees, you see the brilliant aqua color of the ocean ahead....

You walk out of the forest and onto a long stretch of white sand.... the sand is very soft powder.... imagine taking off your shoes, and walking through the hot, white sand toward the water....

The beach is wide and long....

Hear the waves crashing to the shore.... Smell the clean salt water and beach....

You gaze again toward the water.... it is a bright blue-green....

See the waves washing up onto the sand..... and receding back toward the ocean.... washing up.... and flowing back down..... enjoy the ever-repeating rhythm of the waves...

Imagine yourself walking toward the water.... over the fine, hot sand.... you are feeling very hot....

As you approach the water, you can feel the mist from the ocean on your skin. You walk closer to the waves, and feel the sand becoming wet and firm....

A wave washes over the sand toward you.... and touches your toes before receding...

As you step forward, more waves wash over your feet... feel the cool water provide relief from the heat....

Walk further into the clear, clean water.... you can see the white sand under the water.... the water is a pleasant, relaxing temperature.... providing relief from the hot sun... cool but not cold....

You walk further into the water if you wish.... swim if you want to.... enjoy the ocean for a few minutes..... allow the visualization relaxation to deepen.... more and more relaxed... enjoy the ocean.... Now you are feeling calm and refreshed...

You walk back out of the water and onto the beach…

Stroll along the beach at the water's edge…. free of worries… no stress… calm….. enjoying this holiday….

Up ahead is a comfortable lounge chair and towel, just for you…

Sit or lie down in the chair, or spread the towel on the sand…. relax on the chair or towel…. enjoying the sun…. the breeze…. the waves…..

You feel peaceful and relaxed…. allow all your stresses to melt away….

When you are ready to return from your vacation, do so slowly…. Bring yourself back to your usual level of alertness and awareness…. Keep with you the feeling of calm and relaxation…. feeling ready to return to your day….

Open your eyes, stretch your muscles… and become fully alert… refreshed… and filled with energy.

You can practice this visualization relaxation as often as you wish, to provide a mental vacation whenever you need it. Visualization relaxation is a skill that can be learned; the more you practice, the more skilled you will become and more effectively you will be able to relax using visualization relaxation.

Thank you for completing the Lifestyle Redesign Book aiming to help you build a life that you do not have to escape from. Always remember, you have the power to redesign your life, take your control back and achieve the dreams of your desire. I hope the information in this book is of service and of value to you. If you would like 1:1 coaching sessions, please contact me at.....

You can check out my YouTube channel here:

https://www.youtube.com/@temicharlotteoni/videos

Printed in Great Britain
by Amazon